STRAWBERRY COLORING BOOK

CRYSTAL
COLORING BOOKS

ISBN-13: 978-1548556501
ISBN-10: 1548556505

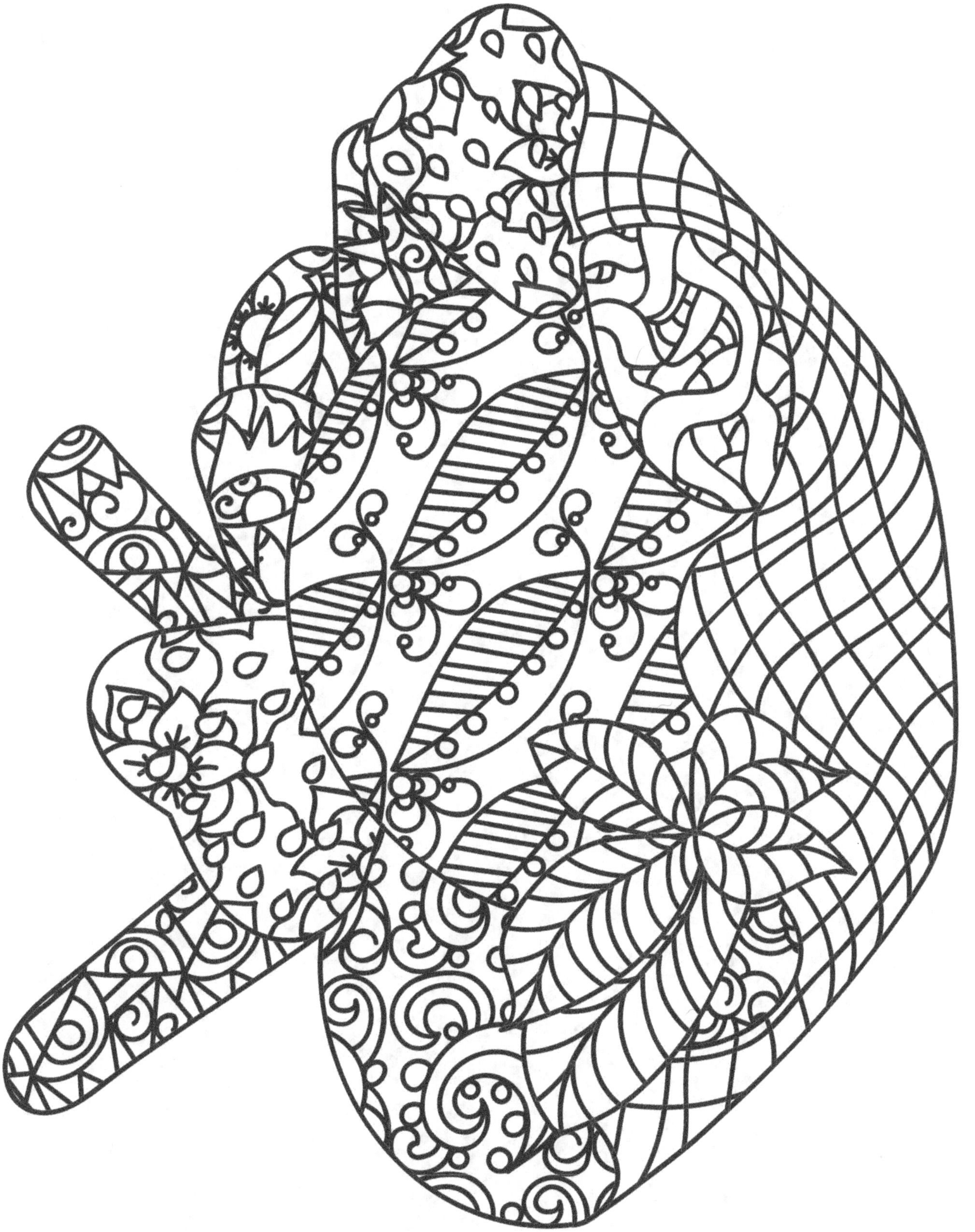

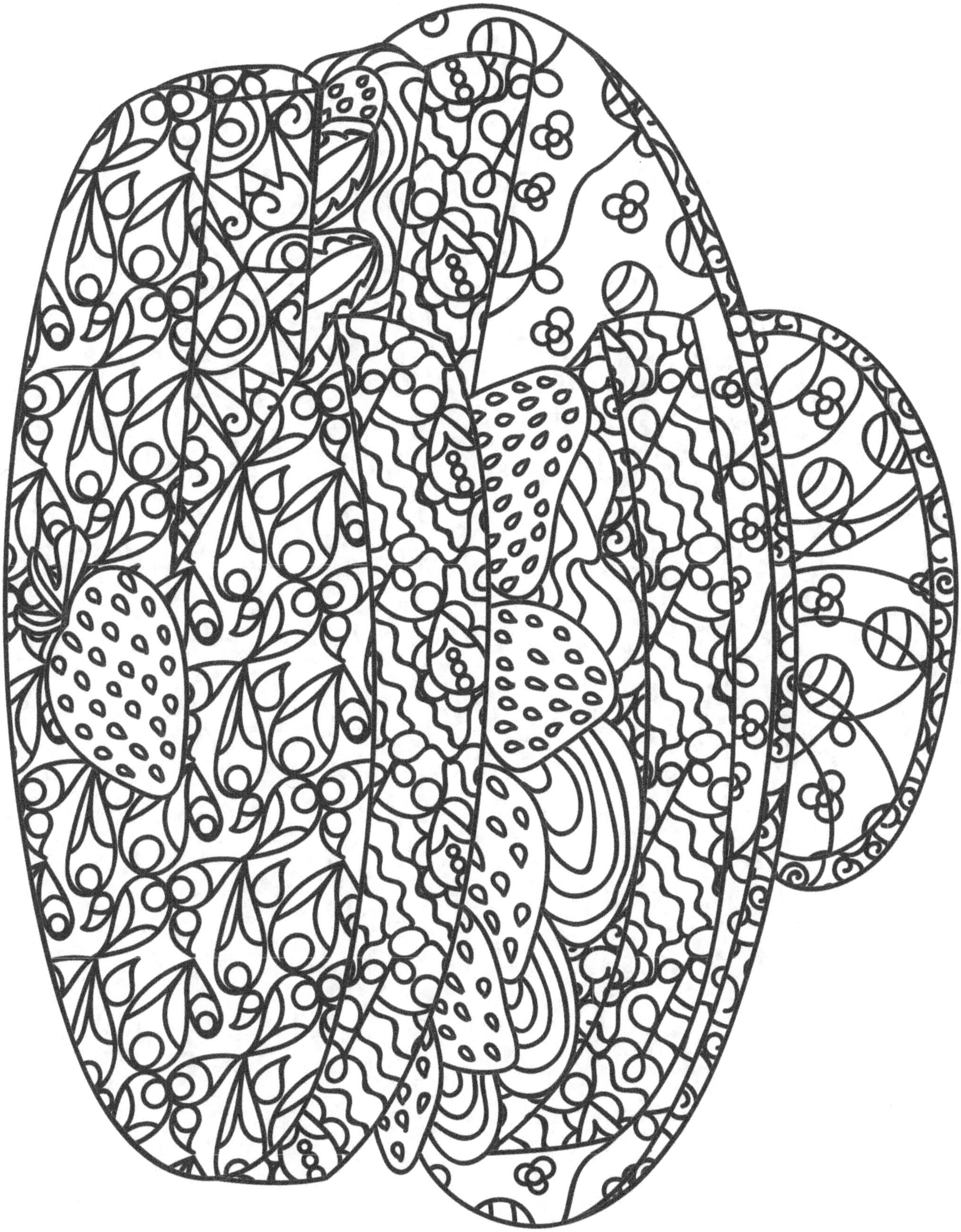

agne

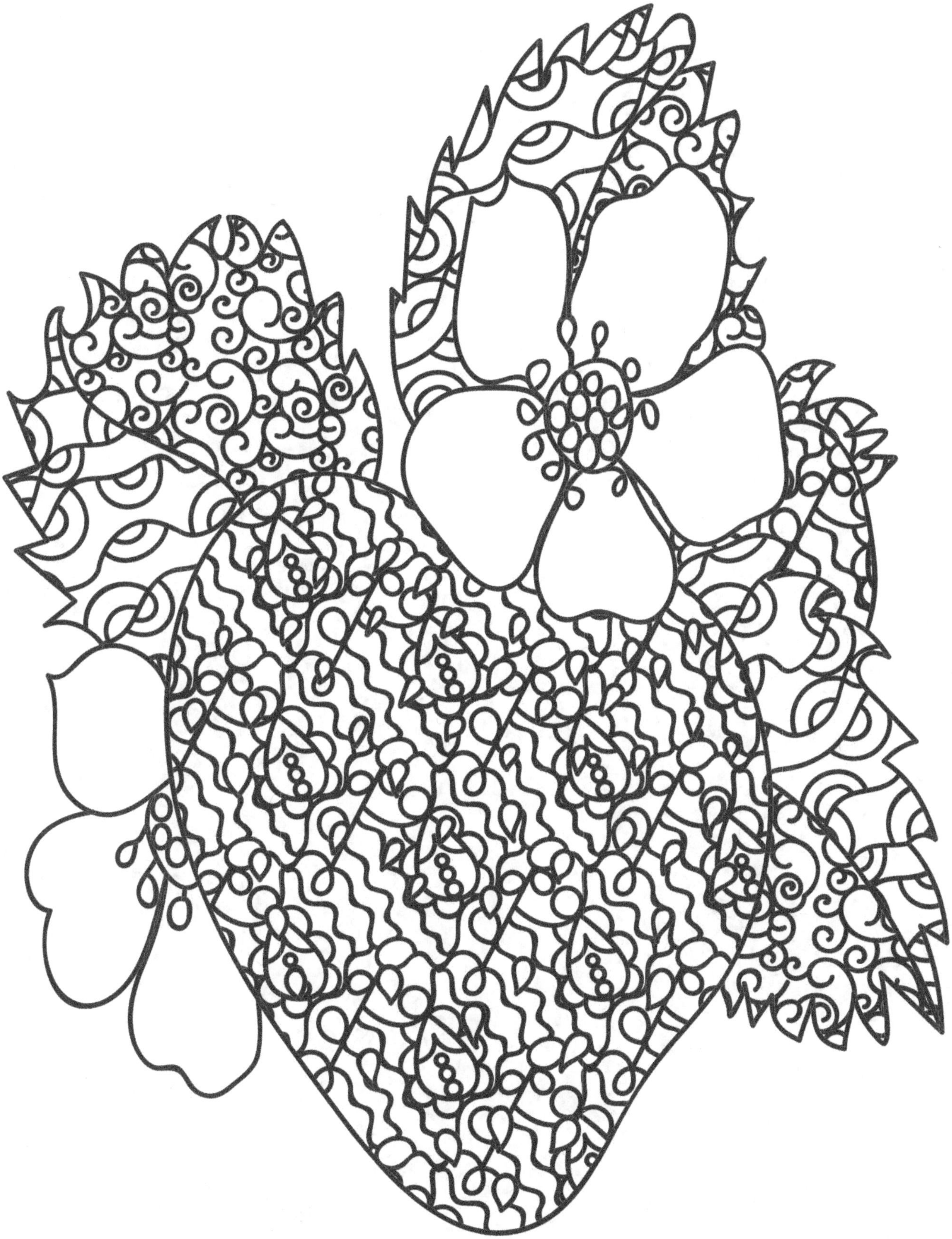

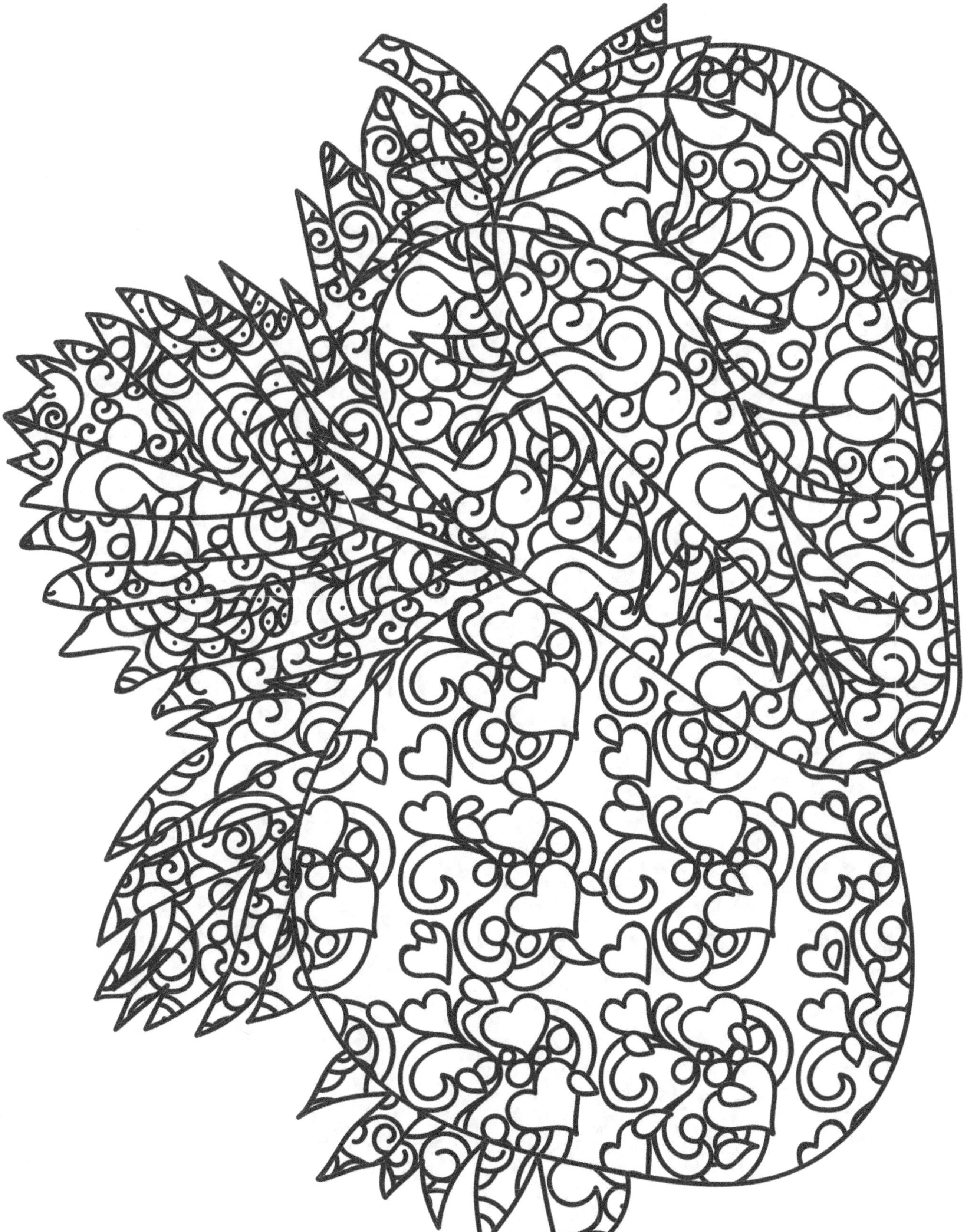

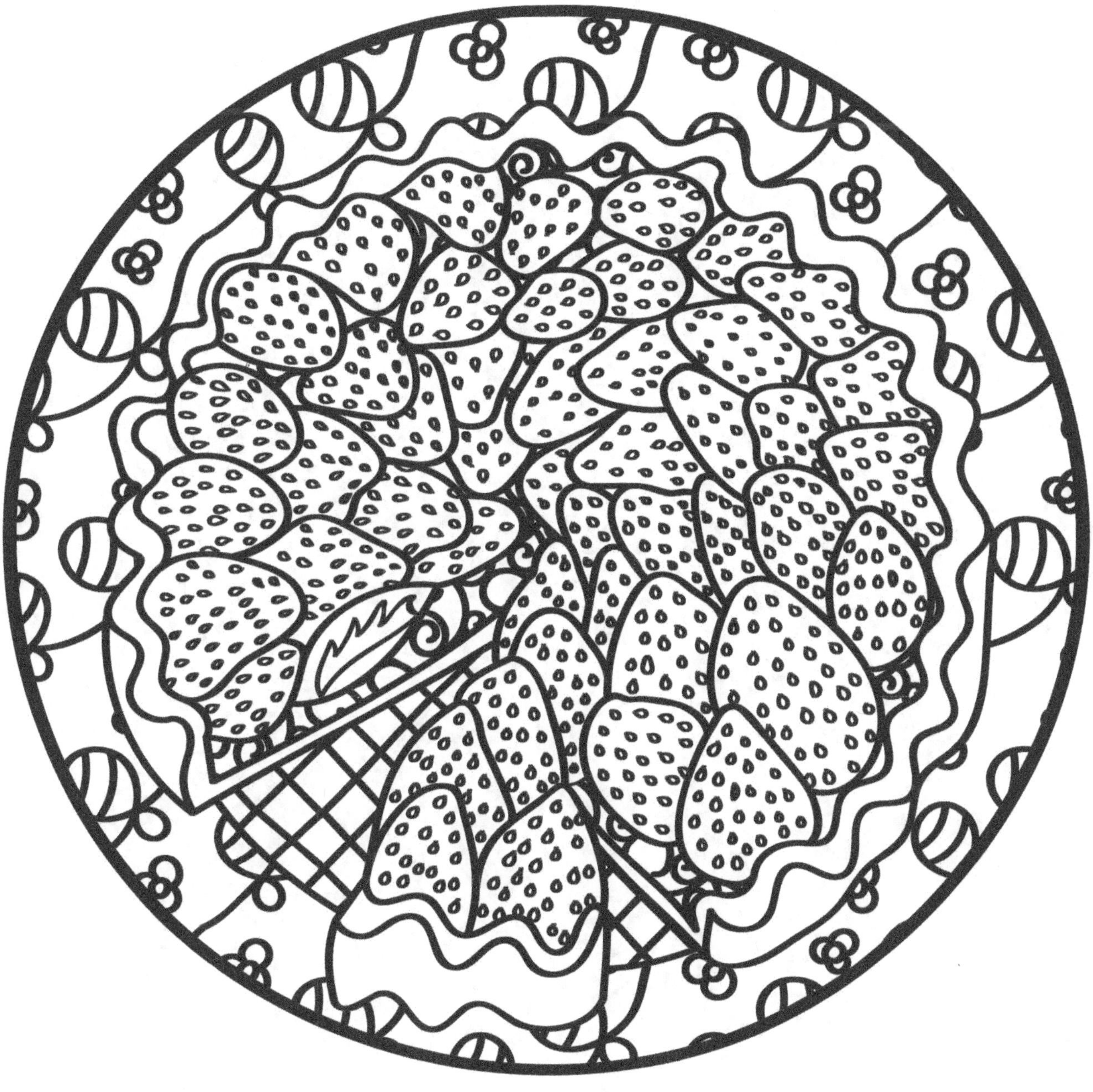

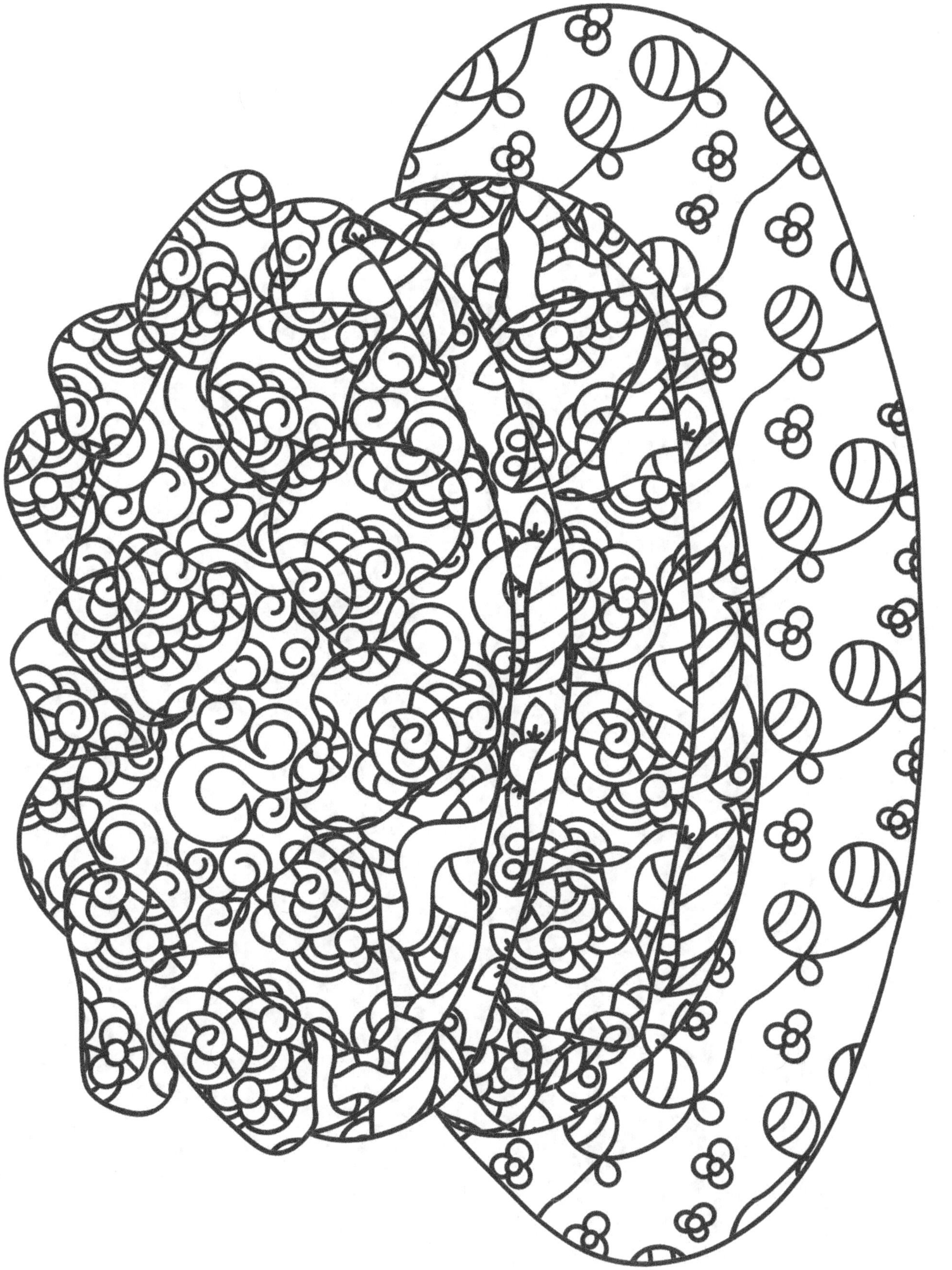

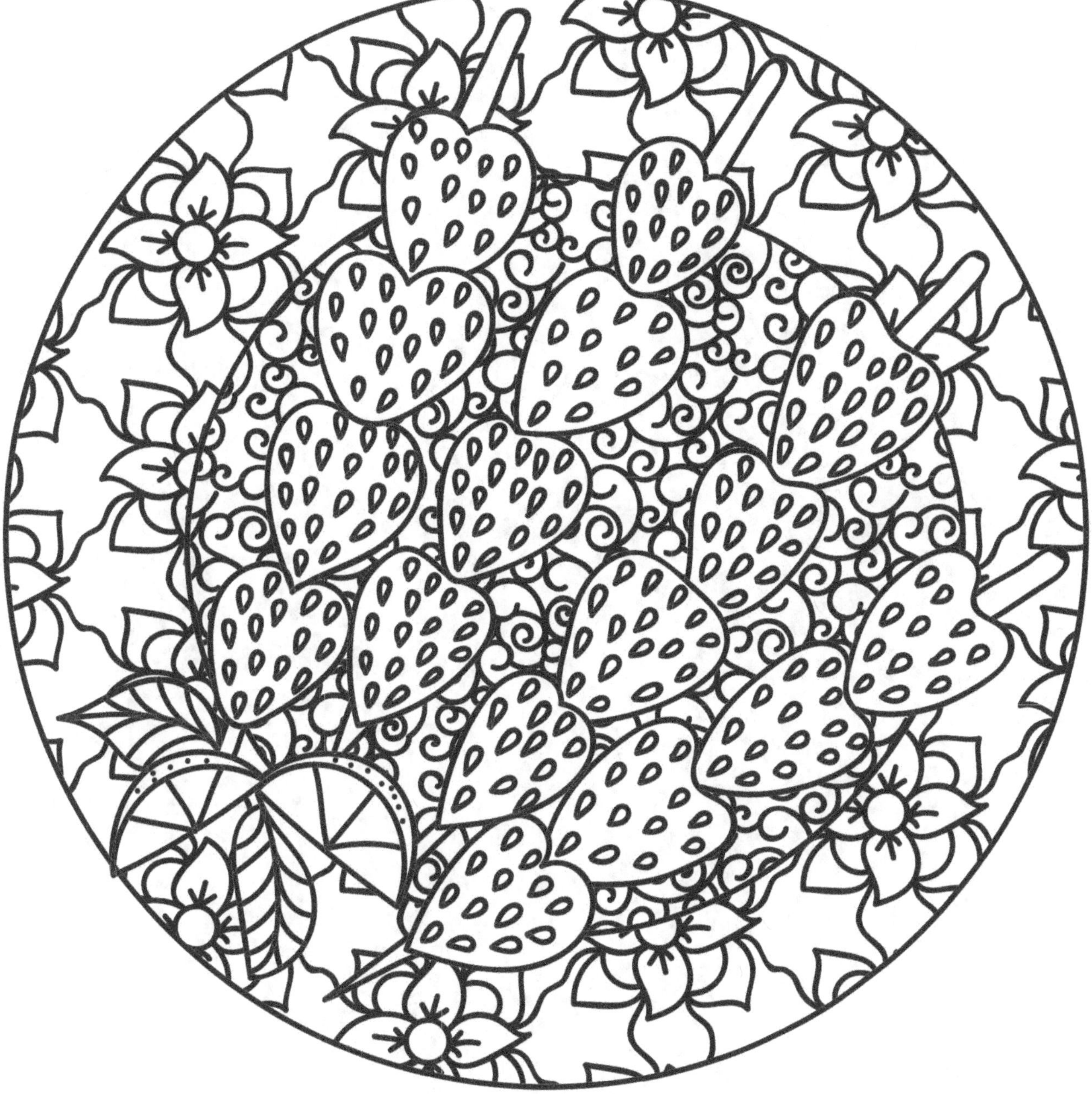

COLOR TEST PAGE

COLOR TEST PAGE

www.ingramcontent.com/pod-product-compliance
Lightning Source LLC
Chambersburg PA
CBHW081244280526
45787CB00006B/2794
* 9 7 8 1 5 4 8 5 5 6 5 0 1 *